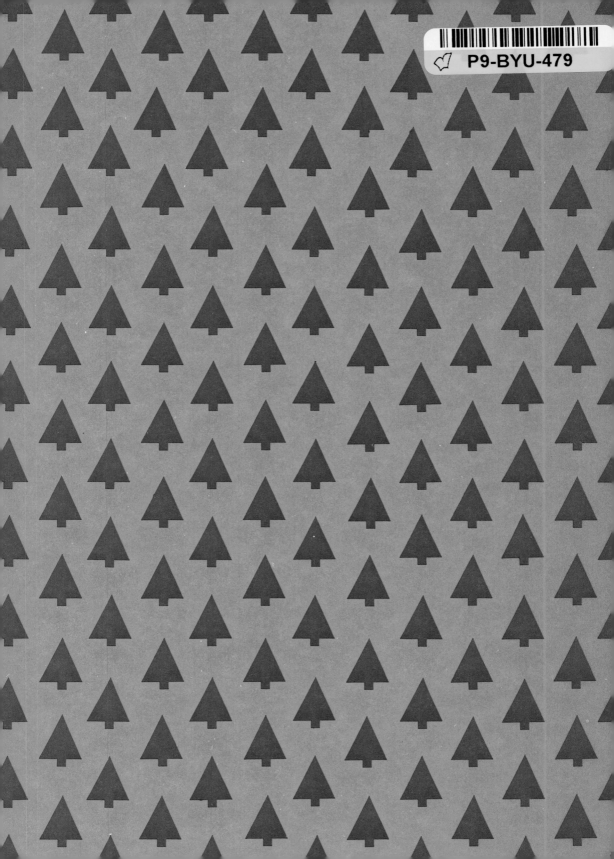

CHRISTMASTIME

CHRISTM

by
Sandra
Baynton

WORKMAN PUBLISHING
NEW YORK

Library of Congress Cataloging-in-Publication Data

Boynton, Sandra.

Christmastime.

1. Christmas—Anecdotes, facetiae, satire, etc.
I. Title.
PN6231.C36B677 1987   818′ .5407   87-6204
ISBN 0-89480-635-1

Book design: Paul Hanson

Workman Publishing Company, Inc.
1 West 39 Street
New York, NY 10018

Manufactured in the United States of America

First printing October 1987

10 9 8 7 6 5 4 3 2 1

The Christmas cards on page 42 were designed by the following artists
(left to right, top to bottom): Wayne Lempka; Gibson Carothers; Robert Keys;
Robert Keys; Gibson Carothers; Audrey Christie; Sandra Boynton;
Margaret McKenna; Annette Kratka; Sandra Boynton.
All copyrights are by Recycled Paper Products, Inc.: © 1984, 1985, 1986.
The cards are reprinted by kind permission of the artists and publisher.

Photograph on page 55 by Walt Chnynwski

The props in the photograph on page 55 were graciously provided by
Garlande Ltd. of Salisbury, Connecticut.

Page 71, ''Santa Claus is Comin' To Town.'' Composer/Arranger:
H. Gillespie & F.J. Coots. © 1934 (RENEWED 1962) LEO FEIST, INC.
All Rights Assigned to SBK CATALOGUE PARTNERSHIP.
All Rights Administered by SBK FEIST CATALOG International Copyright Secured.
Made in USA. All Rights Reserved. USED BY PERMISSION.
Pages 111 and 112, musical arrangement from *Favorite Christmas Carols*
by Charles J.F. Cofone. Used by permission of Dover Publications, Inc., New York, NY.

For My Family, with Love:

Boyntons, Ragsdales, McEwans, Tintles, Steys, Yeichs
Markoffs, Uthuses
and, by fiat:
Capecelatros, Clarkes, Keisers, Newell/Hansons
Stanleys and Wells/Spanos

And particularly to my mother, Jeanne,
for so many wondrous Christmastimes

In religious terms, Christmas is the celebration of the birth of Christ, almost two thousand years ago. More broadly, the season and many rituals adopted in observance of this specific event were appropriated from much earlier pagan festivals—festivals of calling the dying sun back to life and the barren earth back to fruition.

At its center, then, Christmas is a celebration of children, of light and of hope. Christmastime spins somewhat dizzily around this center, often even seeming to obscure it. But my thought with this book was that perhaps I would have a better chance of hitting that center if I didn't aim directly at it.

—S.B.

CONTENTS

INTRODUCTION

GETTING READY FOR THE HOLIDAYS

9

CHAPTER ONE

DECKING THE HALLS

Getting the House Ready 19
Selecting a Tree 24

CHAPTER TWO

CHRISTMAS GREETINGS

Renewing Old Friendships 33
About Christmas Cards 39
The Christmas Newsletter 44

CHAPTER THREE

GIFT-GIVING

The Spirit of Christmas Present. .49
Christmas Shopping 54
Wrapping It Up 60

CHAPTER FOUR

CHRISTMAS TRADITIONS

Keeping Tradition 67
About Santa Claus. 71
A Traditional Holiday Sport 77
Christmas Music 81

CHAPTER FIVE

GOOD THINGS TO EAT

The Christmas Festival 91
Christmas Cookies 93
What's A-Wassailing? 100
About Plum Pudding 102

CONCLUSION

COMING DOWN FROM CHRISTMAS

105

ACKNOWLEDGMENTS 111

One of the true delights of Christmastime is having bought someone just the right gift.

Another is having bought someone just the wrong gift.

INTRODUCTION
GETTING READY FOR THE HOLIDAYS

Christmas comes only one day a year, on December 25. But <u>Christmastime</u> is much longer, starting when the stores put up their Christmas displays

and ending on January 1st, when everyone joyfully welcomes in the new year, and then regrets it.

Because the Christmas season is so drawn-out, it's sometimes hard to sustain the excitement of the holidays right up to Christmas Day.

GIVE ME AN S !
GIVE ME AN A !
HOW 'BOUT AN N ?
LET'S HEAR A T ! ...

Some of us get exhausted and dispirited; others respond to the frenzy of the season by becoming overwrought.

Santaclaustrophobia

And even the efforts of our closest companions to cheer us up somehow only seem to make matters worse.

The best way to avoid fatigue, panic or depression is to try to keep in mind that Christmas is intended to be a celebration, not a contest.

Try to let go of the unrealistic expectations that besiege you. Keep your Christmas preparations simple and rewarding. You might most enjoy decorating a tree

or going caroling with friends.

Si-i-lent night! Ho-o-ly night! All

There are those who like to deck themselves out in holiday finery

and there are those who take great pleasure in keeping up appearances.

Let's see now...ahem:

"Dear Friends,
It has been another hectic year for the indefatigable Van Torvalds. We had no sooner finished celebrating young Matthew's victory at Henley when we received word of Myra's election to the Yale Law Review..."

Some of us enjoy not enjoying Christmas.

And some of us are well content simply to be surrounded by our loved ones during the holidays.

Whatever you choose to do in preparation for your own celebration, recognize that you can't possibly do everything. And remember that, if you can maintain a cheerful attitude, getting ready for Christmas can be a celebration in itself.

A CONSUMER TIP

A tree looks much smaller outdoors than indoors. Be sure to measure both your ceiling height and your prospective tree <u>before</u> you buy it.

CHAPTER ONE

Decking the Halls

GETTING THE HOUSE READY

When does Christmastime at home begin? In spirit, it begins with the decorating of the house; the actual date of this annual ritual varies from household to household. In many families, Christmastime starts as soon as Thanksgiving is over.

Other families find December 1st a logical starting point, and so begin their Christmastime decorating with the hanging of an Advent calendar, and the ceremonial opening of the door marked "1"

often followed by a sneak preview of 2 through 25.

A few staunch traditionalists refuse to decorate their homes until December 24, and some even leave the trimming of the tree to Santa Claus, as if he didn't have enough to do already.

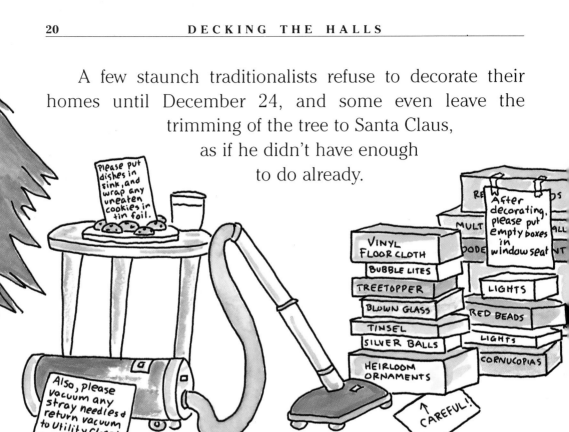

Those who wait until Christmas Eve to do their decorating have a better chance of truly celebrating Christmas, rather than belaboring it. Children in these families have their own special way of showing how much they really appreciate this simpler approach to the holiday.

... and Madeline Fraser already has TWO trees AND an electric Santa Claus, and Benjy Fox has a HUMONGOUS tree with lights that go on and off, and Cynthia Muyskens has a purple shiny tree of her very own, and Nellie MacIntyre has different color candles in every single window of the house, and Clark Szydlow has...

Every household not only has its own starting time for the Christmas season, but also its own distinct style and philosophy of decorating. There are those who tend toward understated elegance

and those who feel that every stationary object cries out for embellishment.

Regardless of their differences in taste and tradition, families the world around get terrifically involved in their Christmas preparations. It's not unusual for people to go about their holiday decorating chores humming, laughing, singing, or softly muttering under their breath.

ANOTHER CONSUMER TIP

When shopping for a Christmas tree, be aware that your tree may have been chopped down a while before you actually purchase it.

And if your cut tree is not really fresh, it may tend to shed its needles too easily.

SELECTING A TREE

It is a common custom for a family to have a decorated evergreen tree in their home throughout the Christmas season. Most people buy their trees already cut, from an enterprising professional.

Cut trees are sold "by the foot,"* and an average-height tree, at $4⁰⁰ a "foot," costs "an arm and a leg."

*1 Christmas Tree Foot = 3 conventional inches

Discouraged by the cost and uncertainty of buying a cut tree, and persuaded by the irrefutable arguments of avid environmentalists

more and more people these days are looking for creative alternatives to the standard practice of chopping down defenseless evergreens for use as Christmas trees.

A number of families have found that with careful lighting and decoration, they can achieve much the same effect as a tree

—although there is usually at least one dissenting reactionary in every family.

Another alternative is to invest in a plastic tree, which can be stored during the year and, at holiday time, assembled in minutes.

Though quite expensive initially ($65^{00} and up), a plastic tree will last many years and can be passed on to the next generation, if they have no taste either.

A third possibility is the inflatable tree. This is an artificial tree made of vinyl sheets that have been preprinted with ornaments. It can and should be blown up. This tree is especially advantageous in homes where space is at a premium, or where Santa Claus is expected to be particularly generous.

NOTE: Inflatable trees are impractical for households with skittish felines.

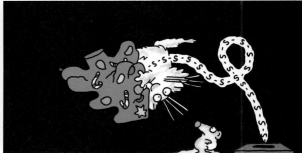

Perhaps the most tasteful and ecologically-sound choice is the living Christmas tree.

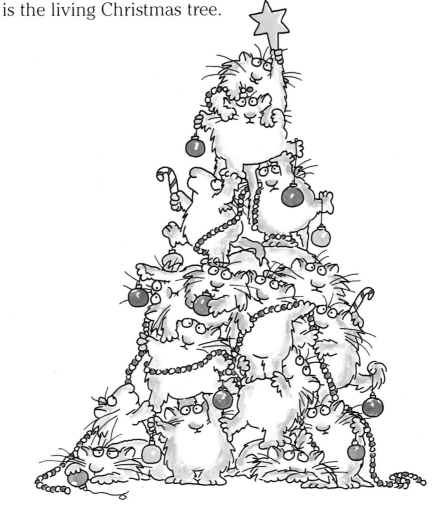

Although stunning in its natural beauty, this type of tree is very difficult to maintain indoors. It needs to be fed and watered three times a day and must be taken outside often. Even with the most painstaking care, the tree may be temperamental and refuse to hold its shape.

Of course, you could always just decorate a tree outside—though this, too, is not without its pitfalls.

If you do, finally, decide on the traditional cut tree, the best one to get would be one that has a sturdy, straight trunk and only one point at the top; that is uniformly full and well-shaped; that has a lusty dark green color; that has soft needles that won't gouge your arm when you try to string the lights; that needs water only twice a week, and will not lose any needles until late January.

If there were such a tree, they would certainly sell a lot of them.

Christmas is the ideal time to contact those individuals that you haven't gotten along with in the past—

—just to let them know that you're still thriving.

CHAPTER TWO

Christmas Greetings

"Narrow isthmus and a zappy Bluebeard".?

RENEWING OLD FRIENDSHIPS

Christmastime is the season for getting back in touch with friends and relatives far and near. There are those who take on the challenge with zest

and there are those of us who think the first sort are compulsive and smug and probably don't have enough to do and maybe are even trying to make us look bad by comparison.

As an alternative to writing cards to all your friends, you could simply telephone them—

—although it's hard to have a spontaneous conversation when you're concerned about the expense.

You could assign the card-writing task to someone who can imitate your handwriting. After all, how would anyone ever know that you didn't do it yourself?

A few energetic souls believe that it's worth the extra effort to convey their good wishes in person.

And there are many less energetic souls who think the effort possibly greater than the rewards.

Perhaps the best thing to do is to approach your card-writing systematically: Beginning on November 29, start with "A" in your address book, and do a letter of the alphabet each day. If you are diligent and disciplined, you'll find that your card-writing is completed on Christmas Eve. But if you are, instead, normal, you'll find someday that the only friends you've kept up with over the years are those whose last names start with A or B or C or D.

Maybe it's best not to even try to get in touch with everyone you know at Christmastime.

Why not write only to your very best friends, and put off writing to everyone else until a more convenient time? Such as next Christmas.

Christmas cards make a wonderful decorative garland. But don't forget to respond to the cards <u>before</u> you hang them up.

ABOUT CHRISTMAS CARDS

Unlike so many holiday products that are motivated solely by cynical profit-making, Christmas cards are purely a public service provided cheerfully by benevolent greeting card companies. Card manufacturers price their cards to just cover expenses, plus enough left over for them to buy Christmas gifts for their own families.

Whereas everyday and special occasion cards are sold individually, Christmas cards are most often *boxed cards,* sold 20 to a box, with 17 or so envelopes.

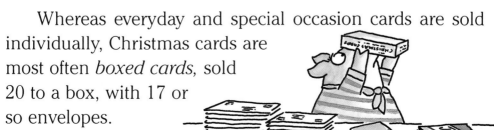

Boxed cards range in price from 4\underline{^{00}}$ a box to 50\underline{^{00}}$, depending on the size and elaborateness of the cards.

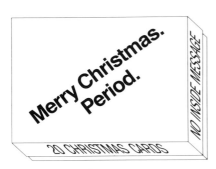

4\underline{^{00}}$ box
(actual size shown)

50\underline{^{00}}$ box
(scale: 1 inch = ½ foot)

Christmas *postcards* are also available in packages. They are comparatively inexpensive, have blessedly little room for writing messages, and allow senders to save on postage as well. Postcards are a good choice for the economy-minded consumer who doesn't have anything particularly private to say to anyone.

A third choice is the *individualized holiday photocard.*
These cards are available from almost any film-processing
business. Photocards come preprinted with a festive sea-
sonal greeting, and most processors will add your family's
names at no extra charge. Envelopes are included, the price
is reasonable, service is quick, reproduction quality is good,
and—best of all—there is absolutely <u>no</u> room on the
cards for additional writing. The only thing you have to do is
provide a photograph of your family that you think is worthy
of being reproduced 25 to 200 times.

Clearly, then, the disadvantages of photocards far outweigh
the benefits.

Choosing the Christmas card you want to send is no simple matter, for your card is a reflection of you. You must decide what image, what taste and style, you want to project. The Christmas card you select as your personal greeting can say "traditional"

"irreverent"

"devout"

"sincere"

"light-hearted"

"sentimental"

"witty,
stylish,
and
intelligent"

"cute"

"fashionable"

"classy"

or "efficient."

MERRY CHRISTMAS,

HAPPY NEW YEAR,

GET WELL SOON,

HAPPY BIRTHDAY,&

MANY THANKS.

If you decide to <u>make</u> your own cards instead of buying them, you will project Creativity, Individuality, Resourcefulness and a Reverence for Tradition

Horse-drawn carriage, c. 1880

as well as an Appalling Lack of Consideration for Professional Greeting Card Artists, Who Have to Make Our Living Somehow, You Know.

THE CHRISTMAS NEWSLETTER

There are people who believe that they have so many close friends that they cannot possibly write an informative letter to everyone. Some solve this problem by simply signing their names.

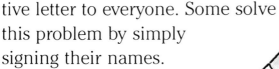

Others are reluctant to deprive their friends of fascinating updates. In the interest of efficiency and egotism, these people compose "Christmas Newsletters" and send a copy to everyone.

Should you find yourself with too many friends and too little time, you may want to try your hand at writing a Christmas newsletter this year. If you are intimidated by the idea of writing fiction for a hostile public, you can use the Model Christmas Newsletter below. This way you can save time and trouble this year <u>and</u> end up with fewer friends next year.

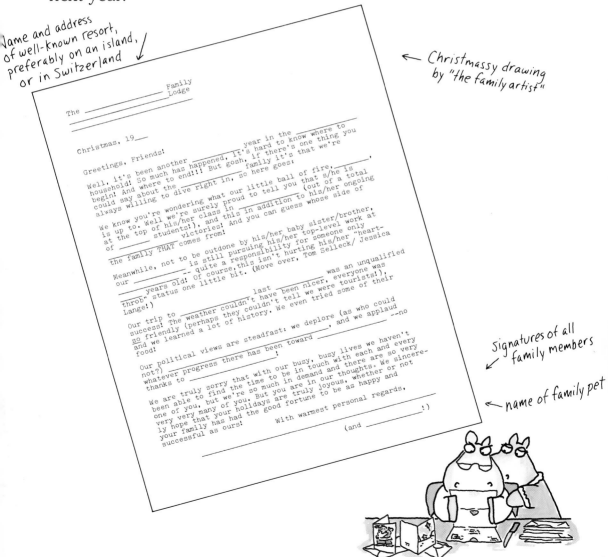

Name and address of well-known resort, preferably on an island, or in Switzerland ↓

← Christmassy drawing by "the family artist"

```
                        _____ Family
                                 Lodge
    The _____
        _____

Christmas, 19___

Greetings, Friends!

    Well, it's been another _____ year in the _____ where to
household! So much has happened, it's hard to know where to
begin! And where to end!!! But gosh, if there's one thing you
could say about the _____ family it's that we're
always willing to dive right in, so here goes:
    We know you're wondering what our little ball of fire, ____,
is up to. Well we're surely proud to tell you that s/he is
at the top of his/her class in _____ (out of a total
of _____ students!), and this in addition to his/her ongoing
_____ victories! And you can guess whose side of
the family THAT comes from!
    Meanwhile, not to be outdone by his/her baby sister/brother,
our _____ is still pursuing his/her top-level work at
_____ -- quite a responsibility for someone only
_____ years old! Of course, this isn't hurting his/her "heart-
throb" status one little bit. (Move over, Tom Selleck/ Jessica
Lange!)
    Our trip to _____ last _____ was an unqualified
success! The weather couldn't have been nicer, everyone was
so friendly (perhaps they couldn't tell we were tourists!),
and we learned a lot of history. We even tried some of their
food!
    Our political views are steadfast: we deplore (as who could
not?) _____, and we applaud _____ --no
whatever progress there has been toward _____!
    We are truly sorry that with our busy, busy lives we haven't
been able to find the time to be in touch with each and every
one of you, but we're so much in demand and there are so very
very very many of you. But you are in our thoughts. We sincere-
ly hope that your holidays are truly joyous, whether or not
your family has had the good fortune to be as happy and
successful as ours!
                           With warmest personal regards,

                    _____

                           (and _____!)
```

Signatures of all family members ↙

← name of family pet

YET ANOTHER CONSUMER TIP

Before you place your gift order with any mail-order catalog company, make sure they have a policy of NO UNAUTHORIZED SUBSTITUTIONS.

CHAPTER THREE

Gift-Giving

2-246-WH	BORDELA, SIDNEY NEW YORK, NY, USA	NAUGHTY
1-460-TF	BORDELAISE, MONIQUE CAEN, FRANCE	NICE
5-673-TY	BORDRACHER, HERMINE HEIDELBERG, W GERMANY	NICE
8-980-JW	BORG, BJORN MONTE CARLO, MONACO	NAUGHTY
8-564-PL	BORNELLO, CONSUELA TOLEDO, SPAIN	NICE
6-878-KM	BORP, SUE TOLEDO, OHIO, USA	NAUGHTY
9-453-YH	BORRICINI, LUIGI VENICE, ITALY	NAUGHTY
3-089-PZ	BORVILLE, ORVILLE M ACKWORTH, ENGLAND	NICE
7-854-OJ	BORZHEVSKI, SVIATOSLAV MOSCOW, USSR	NICE
3-087-EF	BOSA, NOVA SAO PAOLO, BRAZIL	NICE
4-323-ID	BOSBY, MARGARET LONDON, ENGLAND	NAUGHTY
0-965-LK	BOSCH, HIERONYMUS 'S HERTOGENBOSCH, NETHRLDS	NAUGHTY
5-845-LP	BOSCO, URSULA HERSHEY, PA, USA	NICE
8-657-HG	BOSCZYK, SIGISMUND KRAKOW, POLAND	NAUGHTY
4-980-OU	BOSDORE, KARL SALZBURG, AUSTRIA	NICE
7-	P, HEINZ FURT, W	NAUGHTY
	ERING, EY,	NICE
	USA	NAUGHTY
	R	TY
		NICE
9-111-BN	BREEN, MARGOT NANTUCKET ISLAND, MA, USA	NAUGHTY
2-487-DP	BUTHAR, EDWARD ADDIS ABABA, ETHIOPIA	NICE

THE SPIRIT OF CHRISTMAS PRESENT

One of the great joys of Christmastime is giving gifts to those you love.

Among the lesser joys of Christmastime are thinking of

shopping for

and affording

gifts for those you love.

And not even in the running for Joys-of-Christmastime status are thinking of, looking for, and affording gifts for those you are expected to give things to, love or no love.

Yet you could always choose to forego the "should-give" presents, and decide to only spend your time, thought and money on the "want-to-give" presents. Your pride at having made the honest, rational and courageous choice about gift-giving should sustain you through the loss of your job, wrath of your relatives and the substantial deterioration of mail delivery, trash collection and car servicing throughout the coming year.

If you don't feel that you have the stamina to take the consequences of giving up obligatory gift-buying, yet you still find that your financial resources fall short of your ambitions, you may find that December is as good a time as any to pick a fight with your good friends—

—and then you can apologize sometime in January.

Or you can give away the presents you received last Christmas and never used, as long as you're very careful to remember who they were from.

For those who are nearest and dearest to you, remember that they don't need you to buy them costly gifts from stores. Don't spend more than you can afford: your peace of mind is far more important to those who truly care about you. Recognize that the greatest gift* is to give of yourself.

*Also, the cheapest.

AVOIDING THE TWO MOST COMMON CHRISTMAS-GIFT PITFALLS

From September onward, do not allow your children to watch any television whatsoever.

... and I want the all-new Amazing Lightspeed with his realistic Nuclear Power-chop arm; and I want his fearless sidekick, Muscle Merchin; and I want a My Plastic Pal, a go-with-you-anywhere lifesize playmate with built-in voice-activated sound cassette; and I want...

Keep some undesignated gifts in reserve, for anyone who might have been inadvertently overlooked.

CHRISTMAS SHOPPING

As has always been the case, Christmas shopping isn't what it used to be.

Many people head into the holiday shopping season with serious misgivings, knowing that they are about to confront the numerous discomforts that Christmas shopping entails: the impatient crowds, the tinny music, the gaudy decorations, the vibrating lighting, the whining children, the commercial distortions of tradition, the long lines, the surly sales personnel, the high prices and low quality, the sudden realization of your own insignificance and the futility of all human endeavor, and the parking problems.

"DECK THE MALLS WITH PLASTIC HOLLY, FA-LA-LA

Popular magazines and Christmas craft books would have us believe that <u>making</u> Christmas presents is an economical, practical and fulfilling alternative to shopping.

NOVEMBER/DECEMBER

$3.00

FIT FOR A KING: Making Christmas dinner exactly like George I's.

Ladies' Home Circle Companion

A Christmas of Crafts You Can Make at Home:

- ♥ Crocheted sportscar covers
- ♥ Découpage holiday yacht with quilted topmast
- ♥ Cross-stitch tapestry of Domenico Veneziano's "The Annunciation"

♥ PLUS OUR SPECIAL FEATURE ♥

Christmas Clothes to 'Di' for:

- ♥ Patterns and instructions for identical replicas of the clothes Charles, Diana and their two little princes will wear to "Grandma's" palace.

A Renowned Psychiatrist Tells You:
HOW TO BEAT THOSE RED-AND-GREEN BLUES:
- ♥ Seeing through the insidious myths of Holiday Perfection.

If you lack both the skill to make things and the courage to venture forth once more into the stores, you could try mail-ordering from one of the Christmas catalogs your postman brings.

Mail-ordering has all the convenience and comfort of shopping from your own living room. But before you make that easy toll-free first step, you may want to carefully examine a typical packing slip that arrives with mail-ordered merchandise ↓

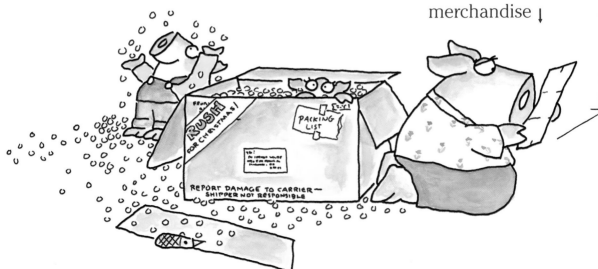

PACKING LIST

ourgeois
of Beverly Hills

" Mail-order House to the Stars "

ORDER #: Z-79305-XL-19528

PACKED BY:
MYRON "BUTTERFINGERS" WATSON

SOLD TO:
Ms. Hester Wilde
440 E. Mt. Pleasant Ave.
Inverness, OH 21098

YOUR VISA CARD HAS
BEEN CHARGED $382.95
FOR THIS ORDER.
HAPPY HOLIDAYS.

N. Seacrest Dr.
wn, Pa.

		SHIP VIA		PAYMENT TYPE		ACCOUNT #		AUTHORIZATION #		
		U P S		VISA		on file		574483		
OF ORDER	SOURCE			EXPECTED	PROCESSING		GIFT	SHIPPING &	TOTAL	
11/23	h 292			SHIP DATE	FEE		WRAP	HANDLING	ITEM PRICE	
#	QUANT.	DESCRIPTION Color Size	STATUS	ITEM PRICE	EXPECTED SHIP DATE	PROCESSING FEE	GIFT WRAP	SHIPPING & HANDLING	TOTAL ITEM PRICE
				45.00	2/25	2.00	2.50	3.00	52.50
4	1	CLOISONNE PEACOCK CUFFLINKS	MFGR's DELAY						
37				70.00	ITEM ENCL.	2.00	4.00	3.50	79.50
06	1	CHIFFON LOUNGING ROBE Blue - W.Large	SUBSTIT. Chartreuse W.Medium						
014				30.00	SUMMER OF '92	2.00	2.50 X 2	3.50	70.50
F19	2	CANVAS LOG-CARRIER W/ DUCK STENCIL	MISLAID IN WAREHOUSE		--	2.00	2.50	3.00	35.50
K86				28.00					
R57	1	SOLAR-POWERED CAN OPENER	ITEM DISCONT. BUT WE CHRGD. YOU FOR IT ANYWY.			2.00	4.00	3.50	61.50
L09				52.00	ITEM ENCL.	2.00			
U94	1	SOAPSTONE SCULPTURE "Unicorn"	SUBSTIT. "Iguana Ballerina						
X77									

SUBTOTAL	299.50
OPERATOR ERROR	25.00
PA. RESIDENTS ADD 7%	15.45
BACKORDER FEE: $3 EA.	6.00
TOTAL	$382.95

A NOTE TO OUR CUSTOMERS

We have made every effort to ensure your complete satisfaction. However, some people are never satisfied. If you wish to return an item:

1. Return it in the original packaging in the same box you received it in, on the same day you receive it.
2. Send it insured, by registered overnight delivery, prepaid.
3. Attach 6 copies of this packing slip, along with a letter explaining the reason for the return, and a 2000-word essay on the decline of Western spiritual values since the Industrial Revolution.
4. You will in due course be issued a credit for the full amount of your purchase (minus processing expenses) that can be used toward the purchase of any item in our catalog.

OUR UNCONDITIONAL GUARANTEE: We promise that every item we sell is backed by this unconditional guarantee.

To Order Additional Merchandise: call toll-free 24 hrs. a day, 7 days a week
1-800-555-0099
WE ARE SORRY, BUT WE CANNOT ACCEPT COLLECT CALLS

FOR BILLING INQUIRIES OR COMPLAINTS, CALL OUR ANCHORAGE ALASKA OFFICE 9 AM–11 AM LOCAL TIME, M—Th

Once you have exploded the myth of carefree Christmas shopping, you will probably resign yourself to braving the stores again this year. Perhaps, then, it's best to realize that the enjoyment of Christmas shopping depends on your approach. Those who think of shopping as a burden inevitably <u>find</u> it a burden.

Those who head off in the firm belief that shopping is a Challenge To Be Met invariably find it stimulating.

And those who look at shopping as a simple, rewarding, joyous pleasure

are a puzzle and an irritation to the rest of us.

FIND THE 8 HIDDEN REINDEER!

WRAPPING IT UP

An hour can be defined as "one-tenth of the time it takes to wrap Christmas presents," and a year can be defined as "the exact amount of time it takes to forget that wrapping all the presents on Christmas Eve is a really bad idea."

But some annual Christmas customs, exhaustion among them, are best let go. At 4 A.M. this coming Christmas morning, take a quick break from your traditional Search for the Scissors

and jot on the October page of your next-year's calendar: "Have all Christmas presents gift-wrapped by stores."

Imagine your calm and satisfaction when Christmas Eve comes around again, and you can relax in the knowledge that everything is already perfectly, beautifully wrapped.

O-0, ti-dings of co-omfort and joy, com-fort and joy...

And imagine your considerable amusement when, late Christmas Eve, it suddenly occurs to you that you didn't label anything, and have no idea what is in any of your perfectly- and beautifully-wrapped packages.

Oh well. Label them as best you can, and go to sleep knowing that you will be as surprised as anyone come Christmas morning.

Buying Christmas Wrap

★ *Two consumer tips for the price of one!* ★

- **READ THE SQUARE FOOTAGE ON THE LABEL**
  Price and roll diameter are unreliable indicators of paper quantity.

- **BEWARE OF EXCESSIVE SQUARE FOOTAGE CLAIMS**
  The <u>weight</u> of the paper is also a factor in true value.

A CHRISTMAS QUIZ

What does Santa Claus say?
   a) Tararaboomdeeay
   b) Where's **MY** present?
   c) Ho ho ho!
   d) Ho ho hum.

Who has a red nose?
   a) The Tooth Fairy
   b) My uncle
   c) Mickey Mouse
   d) Rudolph

Who gets presents from Santa on Christmas?
   a) All the frogs in Utah
   b) Good girls and boys
   c) Pirates and Monsters
   d) Mosquitoes

What do you hang by the chimney on Christmas Eve?
   a) Stockings
   b) Sneakers
   c) Pillowcases
   d) Noodles

What greeting do people use most at Christmastime?
   a) "Hairy Goldfish!"
   b) "What's for dinner?"
   c) "Merry Christmas!"
   d) "I hab ad awfoo code!"

CHAPTER FOUR

Christmas Traditions

It's a long row to ho ho ho.

KEEPING TRADITION

A Christmas tradition is anything that happens every Christmastime, without fail.

Of all the many, many traditions each one of us holds, there is usually one that springs to mind ahead of the rest, as Christmastime approaches. It may be a cherished ornament, a favorite recipe, a family custom, a much-read story, a beloved chorale; it may be the inevitable turkey at Christmas dinner, or it may be the inevitable turkey at the annual office party.

HEY, CUTESTUFF!
Howsabout you and
me splitting this BO-RING
scene for a little HO-HO-HO
and FA-LA-LA-LA-LA?

Some traditions are part of the culture at large, part of our common heritage: Santa Claus, Christmas trees and wreaths, mince pie and eggnog and fruitcake, commercial overkill.

Other traditions are peculiar to one family.

But surely the tradition most common to all who celebrate Christmas is the gathering together of the family. No matter how divergent their paths and how different their lives during the rest of the year, when the members of a far-flung family return home for the holidays, it seems as if nothing has really changed.

ABOUT SANTA CLAUS

"Santa Claus" is the nickname of Saint Nicholas (Saint Nicholas→Sant-Nick-las→Santa Claus.) It is uncertain whether anyone has ever seen Santa Claus himself, even though he is the most widely-impersonated celebrity in the world.

Most of the information we have about Santa comes to us secondhand. Reports of his disposition ("...a right jolly old elf...") and his work ("...Down comes good ol' Santa Claus/ Bringing his presents and lots of toys/ All for the good little girls and boys...") are uniformly positive—notwithstanding the slightly ominous Orwellian cast of the popular song, "Santa Claus is Comin' to Town."

He sees you when you're sleeping, He knows when you're awake, He knows if you've been bad or good.

Because Santa Claus keeps such a low profile, there are certainly those whose prosaic nature prohibits them from believing in him. Try to have as little as possible to do with this sort: anyone who is unable to accept Santa Claus is also likely to be acutely insensitive to those of deeper trust and more perfect imagination.

You know, perhaps one of the most DEVASTATING moments of childhood is when one discovers that there REALLY IS NO SANTA CLAUS.

Throughout the year, Santa makes toys in his workshop, to bring to children while they sleep on Christmas Eve. The actual labor is done by a work force of elves, with Santa Claus acting in a supervisory capacity.

For the most part, Santa's elves are quite content to work without pay and with Santa getting most of the credit for their work. But there are no absolute Utopias.

On Christmas Eve, the elves and Santa Claus load up his sleigh, and he is borne aloft by eight flying reindeer— <u>nine</u> on foggy Christmas Eves.

Or maybe even ten.

Santa Claus then travels the world over, leaving presents at every home that expects him. He enters each house through its chimney

somehow or other.

Since there is so little time between nightfall on Christmas Eve and sunrise Christmas Morning, and so many houses to visit, Santa must use every second wisely. Even so, he almost always finishes the very last house just as day is breaking—

—from whence comes the expression, "Just in the time of Nick!"

HELPFUL HINTS

To keep candycanes from becoming stuck to easy-chair cushions or embedded in your carpeting, either:

1. **DON'T BUY THEM** *or*
2. **DON'T UNWRAP THEM** *or*
3. **DON'T GIVE THEM TO CHILDREN**

To enhance the beauty and extend the indoor life of your Christmas tree:

**ADD ¼ CUP SUGAR TO THE WATER
IN THE TREE STAND**

NOTE: Do not add saccharin, as this will cause your tree to turn to plastic.

A TRADITIONAL HOLIDAY SPORT

A fruitcake is a heavy, dark object 10″ in diameter and 3″ deep, that is wrapped in brandy-soaked linen and encased in a decorative circular tin. Tin and cake together comprise the large "puck" that is used in the popular holiday game, "Pass the Fruitcake." Here's how to play:

The game starts with one team's delivery of the fruitcake to their opponents' house. At least one player on the receiving team must feign delight

while the rest of the team discusses where they should pass the cake.

The object of the game is to get rid of the cake as soon as possible without eating or discarding it, and WITHOUT BEING DISCOVERED BY THE SENDING TEAM. The sending

team may drop in unexpectedly at any time, to check if the cake is still there.

If the receiving team is discovered NOT to have the cake, they must then make a plausible excuse, without actually lying

Well, you can hardly expect to send a CAKE LIKE THAT and have it stay around very long!

—which will of course cause them to receive another fruitcake from
the sending team.

Because no one feels about these cakes the way that you do! Merry Christmas again —
The Rossiters

The first team to be taken in by the fruitcake's uncanny superficial resemblance to edible food —i.e. to "bite"—loses.

TWEEEEEE!

If no one has "bitten" by January 1, the team holding the cake must puncture it, soak it with heated brandy, and bury it in powdered sugar in its tin. The cake is then put away until the following December 1, when the holding team volleys it to another household, and the game resumes.

Yule Never Guess!

HOW MANY OF THESE CHRISTMASTIME PEOPLE, PLACES AND PHRASES CAN YOU IDENTIFY?

A.

...urposes of this agreem...
...e understood to mean a di...
...age of adult age, and of a s...
...ceed two (2) feet in height, i...

...unauthorized person, corporation or...
...r the heirs nor assigns of such pers...
...oration or entity, shall, without pri...
...n permission, represent, impersonate...
...aim to be the true Father Christmas.

...reindeer engaged on a full- or pa...
...s for the purposes of transporti...
...entioned Santa Claus and his...
...solicited parcels by means...
...to a aeronautically-ad...

B.

DECEMBER 25

C.

..You ain't nothin' but a REIN-DEER,
Flyin' all the time..
You ain't nothin but a REIN-DEER,
Flyin' all the time...

D.

EPHANT   CAM

E.

F.

ABOUT CHRISTMAS STOCKINGS

The Christmas Eve tradition of hanging stockings by the fireplace comes from a 4th century legend, wherein then-Bishop Nicholas is said to have anonymously given dowry money for the three daughters of an impoverished merchant, by throwing a bag of gold down their chimney; the gold is said to have landed in the young women's stockings that were hanging there to dry. Nowadays, Santa Claus fills stockings with small presents, nuts, and candy instead of gold, so as not to play havoc with the world economy.

Some acquisitive people hang an unusually large stocking, hoping that Santa Claus will have to use a great number of presents to fill it. When this happens, Santa will usually stuff the stocking with bulky fruit.

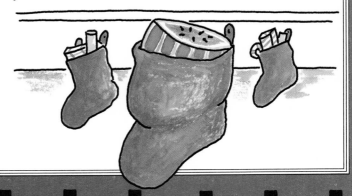

CHRISTMAS MUSIC

There is music around us throughout the year, but somehow the music of Christmastime is particularly captivating —at times, even downright imprisoning.

...ELEVEN pipers piping,
TEN lords a-leaping,
NINE ladies dancing,
EIGHT maids a-milking,
SEVEN swans a-swimming,
SIX geese a-laying,

FIVE GO-OLD
RINGS!!!

FO-OUR calling
birds...

For many centuries, people only had access to music in two ways: the sacred or *liturgical* music consisted of religious chants, hymns and instrumental pieces, and was confined to church; and the worldly or *secular* music was made up of folk songs and dances, which people performed socially among themselves. Christmas *carols* evolved from a blending of the two —sacred imagery set to popular music.

With the invention of the phonograph in the late 19th century, people begun to have access to recorded music as well as live music, and the experience of the sounds of Christmas began to change.

Their Master's Voice

Today, we are constantly being surprised by new and provocative approaches to the traditional music of the holiday season.

There are even innovative greeting cards that play familiar Christmas music when opened, and are pushing the very boundaries of what we mean by "music."

But for all its variety, recorded music can never replace the tradition of singing that has always been so central to the celebration of Christmas. The reasons for making music together are as compelling now as ever, whether it be inspiration,

There's NO business like SNOW business...

nostalgia,

...Christ-mas-time in old Ver-mont...

or a heartfelt desire to reach out to one's neighbors.

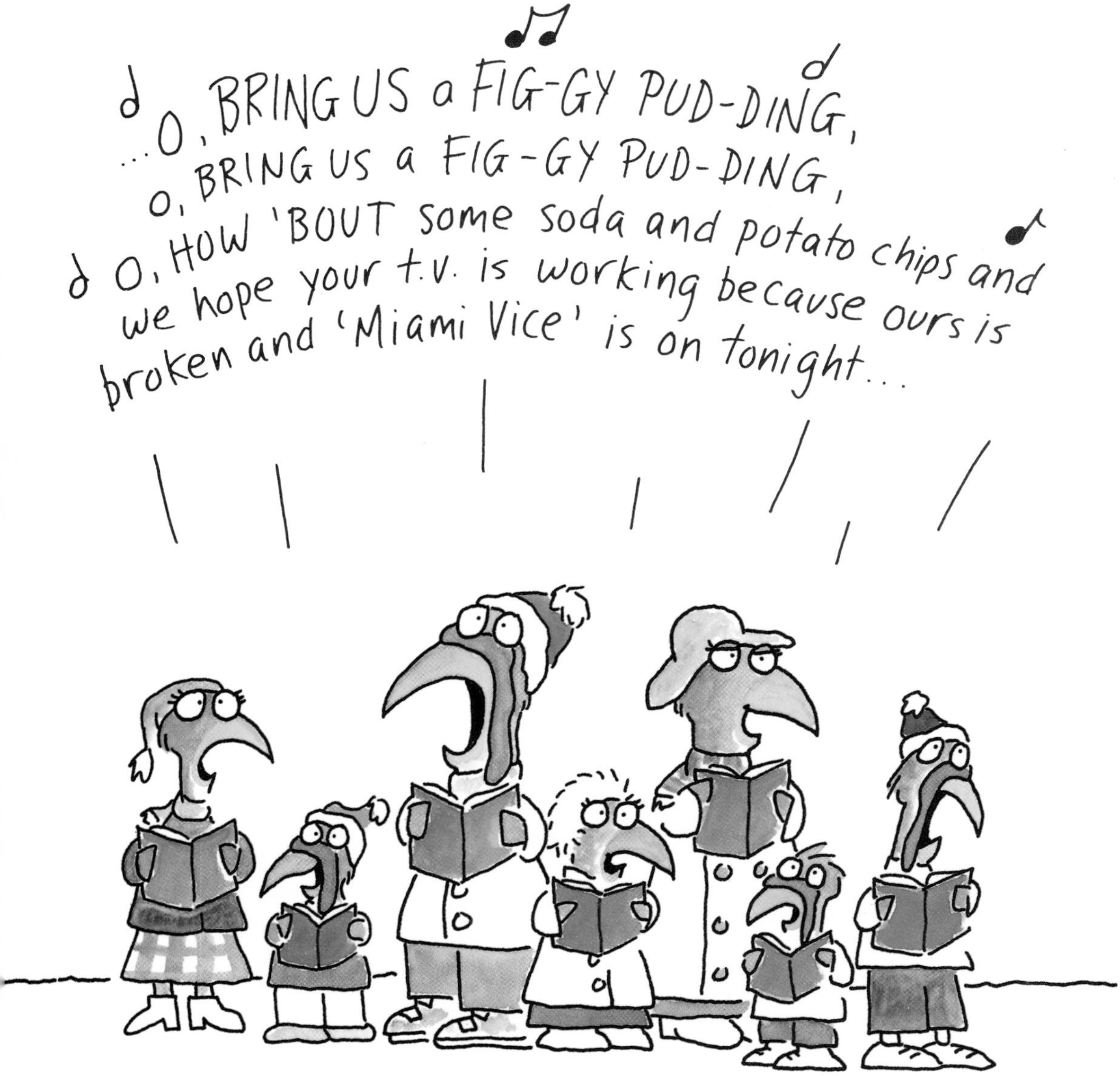

At its best, Christmas music serves to bring us together, to unite us in a common purpose of joyful celebration, to allow us to transcend, for a time, our own corporeal nature and share in a glorious harmony of spirit.

In many homes, a *crèche* is displayed each Christmastime as a simple image of the Nativity.

In homes with young children, the imagery often becomes more complex and eclectic.

Traditionally, a plum pudding
must be steamed for hours.

CHAPTER FIVE

Good Things to Eat

D E C E M B E R
PERSONALITY OF THE MONTH

SANTA "ST. NICK" CLAUS

AGE: 1,706

RESIDES: North Pole

PROFESSION: Part-time Philanthropist

MOST INFLUENTIAL BOOK: Spiegel Catalog

QUOTE: "I think it's not so important what others say about you, as long as you truly believe in yourself."

DRINK: About 60 million glasses of milk every December 24.

THE CHRISTMAS FESTIVAL

Christmas is celebrated in many lands, in many ways. It is sometimes difficult for us to fathom the Christmas rituals practiced by nations whose language and culture are vastly different from ours —particularly the food rituals. Imagine, for example, an apparently civilized country where the natives keep Christmas by eating the heads of wild boars, by drinking from ceremonial vessels a warm ale-and-egg brew, and by setting fire to sweetened mounds of beef loin fat and flour! And yet, for all that, the British are probably people just like us.

No matter where it is celebrated, Christmas is a time of giving gifts and sharing food; of singing songs and drinking toasts; of dancing and dining; of talking and feasting; of visiting and eating and drinking; of eating and eating, and of drinking and drinking.

oof!

desemBer3,,

dEar SAntac ClaUse;

we i mean ive bin THinkingabout howw lucky
you/are to have such nis/ce raindeer. you
get so many cookies &and milk evry year i think
you shoud give a ~~kake~~ whole bunch of themto
those GREat raindeer, ok?? We kids wouldn8t
mind at all becaus those raindeer shure are
great.

LOVe,

a kid

CHRISTMAS COOKIES

Christmas and cookies are practically synonymous.

On the pages that follow, you will find recipes for three different kinds of Christmas cookies that are delicious and easy to make. A very special Christmas gift is a box-, basket-, or tinful of cookies you've baked yourself.

Then again, a box or basket or tin makes a very nice gift all on its own.

COOKIE-CUTTER COOKIES

Every family has a box of cherished cookie cutters that are brought out every Christmastime and pressed into service. These are the most traditional shapes:

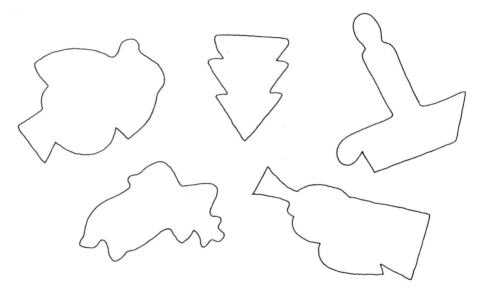

Some folklorists believe that these shapes originally had some representational significance, but no one has as yet been able to offer a plausible interpretation of the cutter symbolism.

The cookies can be eaten plain, or can be decorated before baking with raisins, currants, cinnamon imperials, colored sugar sprinkles, or anything else that can't easily be removed from the cracks in the kitchen table.

ROLLED LEMON COOKIES

Cream together:
- ½ cup white sugar
- ½ cup brown sugar
- 1 cup unsalted (sweet) butter

Beat, then add to the butter mixture:
- 4 eggs
- 2 teaspoons lemon extract
- 1 teaspoon grated lemon peel

Stir in:
- 4 cups all-purpose flour
- 3 teaspoons baking powder

Divide the dough into 3 parts. Wrap and refrigerate at least 4 hours before rolling.

TO ROLL: Use a pastry cloth and rolling pin cover. (Many home bakers use flour to repeatedly cover the rolling pin and the rolling surface to keep the dough from sticking. Unfortunately, this can make for very tough cookies.)

Cut into shapes, and place on a greased, unrimmed cookie sheet. Bake at 375°F, for 8 to 10 minutes. Cool on a rack.

COOKIES FROM GERMANY

There are a great number of cooks who love to try out traditional Christmas foods from other countries

Pfeffernüsse?

Gesundheit!

and a great number of guests who really don't understand foreign food.

Pfeffernüsse are traditional German Christmas cookies. They are white on the outside and dark brown on the inside, rich and spicy and slightly dry. Their name means "pepper nuts"; and "pepper nuts" doesn't mean anything.

PFEFFERNÜSSE

Preheat oven to 375°F.

In a heavy saucepan, bring slowly to a boil:
>   ¾ cup honey
>   ½ cup corn syrup

Let simmer 5 minutes, then add:
>   3 tablespoons unsalted (sweet) butter

Remove from the heat and let cool.

In a separate bowl, sift together, then sift again:
>   3 cups all-purpose flour
>   1 teaspoon baking powder
>   1 teaspoon ground cloves
>   2 teaspoons ground allspice
>   ½ teaspoon ground pepper

In yet another bowl, blend together:
>   1 egg
>   3 drops oil of anise
>   ¾ cup dark brown sugar
>   2 tablespoons grated lemon peel

Add the cooled syrup to the egg mixture. Add the flour mixture ½ cup at a time, stirring constantly.

Shape the dough into 1-inch balls, and press lightly onto greased, unrimmed cookie sheets.

Bake for 12 to 15 minutes. Cool on a rack for 5 minutes, then roll in confectioners' sugar.

COOKIES FOR SANTA CLAUS

Traditionally, families leave out homemade cookies for Santa on Christmas Eve. Some people leave him a whole fruitcake (see page 77), and his appreciation is such that he in turn leaves an identical cake under their tree.

Santa is grateful for any kind of cookie that is left for him, but his favorite is unquestionably Chocolate Chip. On Christmas Eve, leave out a plate of these cookies with a large glass of milk. In a high place.

CHO-HO-HOCOLATE CHIP COOKIES

Preheat oven to 375°F.

Cream together until light:
   ¾ cup unsalted (sweet) butter
   ¾ cup light brown sugar
   ¼ cup dark brown sugar

Beat in:
   1 egg
   1 teaspoon vanilla extract

In a separate bowl, sift together:
   1⅓ cups all-purpose flour
   ¾ teaspoon baking soda

Stir flour mixture into butter mixture.

Chop into pieces, then stir in:
   2 bars (3 ounces each) bittersweet chocolate

Sample the batter.

Drop the remaining batter onto a lightly-greased, unrimmed cookie sheet. Bake the cookies about 10 minutes. Cool on a rack. Maybe you should have doubled the recipe.

WHAT'S A-WASSAILING?

"Wassail!" is a salutation meaning "To your health!" It is also the name of the hot spiced ale that is used, especially in Great Britain, for the drinking of healths at Christmastime. Often there is an ornate silver Wassail Bowl, which is filled with the wassail drink and carried from house to neighbor's house, as the bearers "go a-wassailing."

At each house, a toast is drunk to the health of every member of the household. After the fifth house, toasts are often drunk to the health of the furniture as well.

Some etymologists believe that the word "wassail" comes from the Middle English *"was"* (BE) and *"hail"* (HALE, i.e. in good health). But anyone who has ever been wassailled knows that "wassail" is simply an inebriated contraction of "What's in this ale?" This is what's in it:

WASSAIL PUNCH

Core, halve, and roast:
　120 medium apples

Beat with a wire whisk:
　240 eggs

When you have recovered, pour the eggs into a largish pewter kettle. Add:
　125 gallons ale

Add the apples, and bring to a boil over medium flame. Add:
　1½ gallons molasses
　2 pounds raw sugar
　2,640 blanched almonds
　1 cup grated nutmeg
　1½ pounds ground cinnamon
　½ pound ground ginger
　⅓ bushel whole cloves

Let simmer 2 hours, stirring occasionally.
Serve hot. And often.

ABOUT
PLUM PUDDING

Except for the fact that it's really a cake, not a pudding, and there are no plums in it, "Plum Pudding" is a very aptly-named dish. British in origin, its enjoyment has spread to many other countries, too. Often silver coins and trinkets are baked right into the cake, a custom reputed to have been started and popularized by dentists.

Plum Pudding is a very challenging, time-consuming and expensive dessert to make, but the results are well worth someone else's time and money.

PLUM PUDDING

Withhold from winter songbirds:
> 2½ cups beef suet

Shred the suet very fine, and add to it:
> 1 cup raisins
> 2 cups currants
> Grated peel of 1 lemon
> ½ cup candied orange
> ½ cup candied lemon

In a separate bowl, mix together:
> 2 cups all-purpose flour
> 1¼ cups loosely packed dark brown sugar
> 2 teaspoons ground cinnamon
> 2 teaspoons ground cloves
> 1 teaspoon grated nutmeg
> ½ teaspoon ground ginger

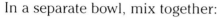

Add to the fruit mixture.

In a separate bowl, beat:
> 3 eggs
> 1 cup milk
> ¼ cup brandy

Add this to the fruit mixture. Put the batter in a cool place, and let stand 12 hours.

TO STEAM THE PUDDING: Transfer the batter to a buttered 2 quart pudding basin. Cover the basin with buttered wax paper, then foil. Tie tightly with string. Place it in a large pot, and pour in boiling water to reach halfway up the basin. Bring water to a gentle boil, and cover the pot tightly. Steam for 4 hours. Add boiling water throughout steaming, to maintain water level. When cool, replace foil and paper top with fresh paper. Store in a cool, dry place.

TO SERVE THE PUDDING: Steam the pudding a second time, for 2 hours. Turn it out onto a serving plate, pour over it 2 tablespoons heated brandy, and ignite.

This is a meal that is traditionally eaten from January 2 through February. Serve with water.

KAROTTENSTICKENDIETETTISCH

Wash and peel:
   24 carrots

Slice lengthwise, and arrange appetizingly on a platter.

CONCLUSION
COMING DOWN FROM CHRISTMAS

Post-Christmas letdown is so commonplace that many of us take it as a given. And yet what we fail to realize is that Christmastime, like any other marathon event, will necessarily be frustrating and exhausting for anyone who has not trained for it properly. Of course, success is never guaranteed, but if you carefully examine your own program of holiday fitness preparation, you may discover effective new strategies for achieving your Personal Best Christmastime.

More often than not, Holiday Blues are the indirect result not of too little preparation, but too much. Here are the three most common training errors:

1. OVERTRAINING

Intensive conditioning is an excellent idea, but it is possible to overdo it. Remember: you can't perform if you're not prepared, but neither can you perform if you're worn out.

2. OVERREACHING

Many people set themselves up for defeat simply by entering Christmastime with unrealistic hopes and expectations.

3. PEAKING TOO SOON

It is not possible to sustain indefinitely the physical and psychological "edge" that a truly successful Christmastime demands. Build up to Christmas gradually, and don't start too early.

But perhaps no matter how well-prepared you are, you're bound to watch the passing of Christmas with some relief, yet some sadness, too. Try as best you can to keep Christmas in your own way, and be willing to let it go when the time comes.

Dependent Claus

And never fear: Christmastime will be back again next year, in all its variety, glory, and confusion.

On DASHER, on DANCER,
on... um... on DASHER and VIXEN!
On COMET, on AJAX, on... um...
DANCER and BLITZEN!
Come CUPID and DONDER
and... and... FLOPSY and IGOR!
On... um... phooey... DASHER and NIXON!
Come... HAPPY, come GRUMPY,
come DOPEY and SNEEZY!
On... oh, dash it all, dash it all,
DASH AWAY ALL!

ACKNOWLEDGMENTS

I would like to thank the following people,
for all their help and good will:

Jeanne and Bob Boynton
Keith Boynton
Jane and Mark Capecelatro
Mary Cooney
Martha Fullington
Paul Hanson
Cathy Hearn
Kathleen Herlihy-Paoli
Mike Keiser
Kate Klimo
Edite Kroll

Caitlin McEwan
Devin McEwan
Suzanne Rafer
Shannon Ryan
Roberta Silverman
Bert Snyder
Geoffrey Strachan
Joanne Strauss
Mary Tobin
Ludvik Tomazic
Peter and Carolan Workman

and most especially:
Jamie McEwan

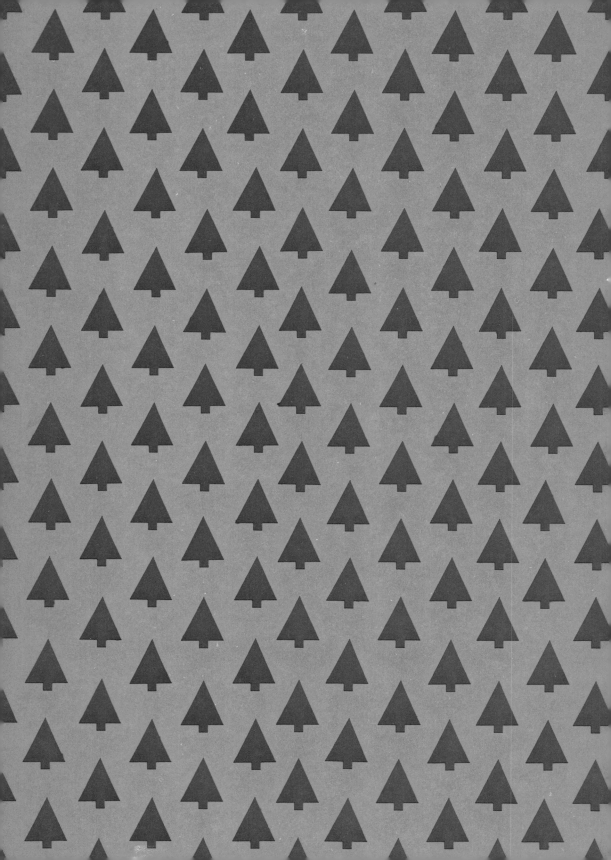